INTRODUCCIÓN

"Python programming is one of the most valuable skills anyone can acquire in the digital age. With clear and readable syntax, Python has become the language of choice for beginners and experts alike. Its versatility and ease of use have made it ubiquitous in a wide range of applications, from web development to artificial intelligence and data science.

This book is designed to take you on an exciting journey through the basics of Python, from zero to a level where you will feel comfortable solving basic-level programming problems. Whether you are a complete beginner or someone looking to solidify their foundations, this book has something for you.

Our approach is based on active practice. As you progress through this book, you will not only learn the theoretical concepts of Python but also apply that knowledge through a series of carefully designed exercises. Each exercise is designed to challenge you, yet at the same time, provide you with a solid and gradual understanding of Python."

CONTENIDO

Input Data Exercises

These exercises cover basic input, calculations, and decision-making in Python, making them suitable for beginners to practice their programming skills.

Exercise 1: Input and Output

Description: Write a Python program that takes a user's name as input and prints a greeting message with their name.

Solution:

```
name = input("Enter your name: ")

print("Hello, " + name + "!")
```

Exercise 2: Simple Calculator

Description: Create a basic calculator that takes two numbers and an operator (+, -, *, /) as input and performs the corresponding operation.

Solution:

```
num1 = float(input("Enter the first number: "))
operator = input("Enter an operator (+, -, *, /): ")
num2 = float(input("Enter the second number: "))
```

```
if operator == "+":
    result = num1 + num2
elif operator == "-":
    result = num1 - num2
elif operator == "*":
    result = num1 * num2
elif operator == "/":
    result = num1 / num2
else:
    result = "Invalid operator"
print("Result:", result)
```

Exercise 3: Calculate Area of a Circle

Description: Write a Python program that calculates and prints the area of a circle given its radius.

Solution:

```
import math

radius = float(input("Enter the radius of the circle: "))
area = math.pi * radius ** 2
print("The area of the circle is:", area)
```

Exercise 4: Temperature Converter

Description: Create a program that converts temperatures from Celsius to Fahrenheit. Take the temperature in Celsius as input and display the equivalent temperature in Fahrenheit.

Solution:

```
celsius = float(input("Enter temperature in Celsius: "))
fahrenheit = (celsius * 9/5) + 32
print("Temperature in Fahrenheit:", fahrenheit)
```

Exercise 5: Check Even or Odd

Description: Write a program that checks whether a given integer is even or odd.

Solution:

```
number = int(input("Enter an integer: "))
if number % 2 == 0:
    print(number, "is even.")
else:
    print(number, "is odd.")
```

Exercise 6: Sum of Digits

Description: Write a program that calculates the sum of the digits in an integer number.

Solution:

```
number = int(input("Enter an integer: "))
sum_of_digits = 0

while number > 0:
    digit = number % 10
    sum_of_digits += digit
    number //= 10

print("Sum of digits:", sum_of_digits)
```

Exercise 7: Reverse a String

Description: Create a program that takes a string as input and prints the reverse of that string.

Solution:

```
string = input("Enter a string: ")
reverse_string = string[::-1]
print("Reversed string:", reverse_string)
```

Exercise 8: Count Vowels in a String

Description: Write a program that counts the number of vowels (a, e, i, o, u) in a given string.

Solution:

```
string = input("Enter a string: ")
vowels = "aeiouAEIOU"
count = 0

for char in string:
    if char in vowels:
        count += 1
print("Number of vowels:", count)
```

Exercise 9: Check Leap Year

Description: Write a program that checks if a year entered by the user is a leap year.

Solution:

```python
year = int(input("Enter a year: "))

if (year % 4 == 0 and year % 100 != 0) or (year % 400 == 0):
    print(year, "is a leap year.")
else:
    print(year, "is not a leap year.")
```

Exercise 10: Simple Interest Calculator

Description: Create a program that calculates the simple interest for a principal amount, rate, and time period provided by the user.

Solution:

```python
principal = float(input("Enter the principal amount: "))
rate = float(input("Enter the annual interest rate (%): "))
time = float(input("Enter the time period (years): "))
simple_interest = (principal * rate * time) / 100
print("Simple Interest:", simple_interest)
```

Strings Exercises

These exercises provide a foundation for working with strings in Python and are ideal for beginners looking to improve their programming skills.

Exercise 1: Greet the User

Description: Write a Python program that takes the user's name as input and prints a greeting message.

Solution:

```
name = input("Enter your name: ")
print("Hello, " + name + "!")
```

Exercise 2: Count Characters

Description: Create a program that takes a string as input and counts the number of characters in it, including spaces.

Solution:

```
text = input("Enter a string: ")
count = len(text)
print("Number of characters:", count)
```

Exercise 3: Reverse a String

Description: Write a program that takes a string as input and prints the reverse of that string.

Solution:

```
text = input("Enter a string: ")
reverse_text = text[::-1]
print("Reversed string:", reverse_text)
```

Exercise 4: Check Palindrome

Description: Create a program that checks if a given string is a palindrome (reads the same forwards and backwards).

Solution:

```
text = input("Enter a string: ")
if text == text[::-1]:
    print("It's a palindrome!")
else:
    print("It's not a palindrome.")
```

Exercise 5: Count Words

Description: Write a program that counts the number of words in a string.
Assume words are separated by spaces.

Solution:

```
text = input("Enter a string: ")
words = text.split()
word_count = len(words)
print("Number of words:", word_count)
```

Exercise 6: Uppercase and Lowercase

Description: Create a program that takes a string as input and prints it in uppercase and lowercase.

Solution:

```python
text = input("Enter a string: ")
uppercase_text = text.upper()
lowercase_text = text.lower()

print("Uppercase:", uppercase_text)
print("Lowercase:", lowercase_text)
```

Exercise 7: Replace Characters

Description: Write a program that replaces all occurrences of a character in a string with another character.

Solution:

```python
text = input("Enter a string: ")
old_char = input("Enter the character to replace: ")
new_char = input("Enter the new character: ")

modified_text = text.replace(old_char, new_char)
print("Modified string:", modified_text)
```

Exercise 8: Extract Substring

Description: Create a program that extracts a substring from a given string, specifying a starting index and length.

Solution:

```python
text = input("Enter a string: ")
start = int(input("Enter the starting index: "))
length = int(input("Enter the length: "))

substring = text[start:start+length]
print("Extracted substring:", substring)
```

Exercise 9: Title Case

Description: Write a program that converts a string into title case (capitalizes the first letter of each word).

Solution:

```python
text = input("Enter a string: ")
title_case_text = text.title()
print("Title case:", title_case_text)
```

Exercise 10: Count Vowels and Consonants

Description: Create a program that counts the number of vowels and consonants in a string.

Solution:

```python
text = input("Enter a string: ")
text = text.lower()
vowels = "aeiou"
vowel_count = 0
consonant_count = 0

for char in text:
    if char.isalpha():
        if char in vowels:
            vowel_count += 1
        else:
            consonant_count += 1

print("Vowels:", vowel_count)
print("Consonants:", consonant_count)
```

Conditionals Exercise

These exercises cover basic conditional statements in Python and are suitable for beginners to practice their programming skills.

Exercise 1: Check Even or Odd

Description: Write a Python program that takes an integer as input and prints whether it's even or odd.

Solution:

```
number = int(input("Enter an integer: "))
if number % 2 == 0:
    print("Even")
else:
    print("Odd")
```

Exercise 2: Find the Larger Number

Description: Create a program that takes two numbers as input and prints the larger number.

Solution:

```
num1 = float(input("Enter the first number: "))
num2 = float(input("Enter the second number: "))
if num1 > num2:
    print("The larger number is:", num1)
else:
    print("The larger number is:", num2)
```

Exercise 3: Grade Calculator

Description: Write a program that takes a student's score as input and prints their grade based on the following criteria:

90 or above: A
80-89: B
70-79: C
60-69: D
Below 60: F

Solution:

```
score = float(input("Enter the student's score: "))
if score >= 90:
    grade = "A"
elif score >= 80:
    grade = "B"
elif score >= 70:
    grade = "C"
```

```
elif score >= 60:
    grade = "D"
else:
    grade = "F"
print("Grade:", grade)
```

Exercise 4: Leap Year Checker

Description: Create a program that checks if a year is a leap year (divisible by 4 and not divisible by 100, except if divisible by 400).

Solution:

```
year = int(input("Enter a year: "))
if (year % 4 == 0 and year % 100 != 0) or (year % 400 == 0):
    print(year, "is a leap year.")
else:
    print(year, "is not a leap year.")
```

Exercise 5: Sign Checker

Description: Write a program that takes an integer as input and prints whether it's positive, negative, or zero.

Solution:

```
number = int(input("Enter an integer: "))
if number > 0:
    print("Positive")
elif number < 0:
    print("Negative")
else:
    print("Zero")
```

Exercise 6: Triangle Type

Description: Create a program that takes three integer angles as input and prints whether they form an equilateral, isosceles, or scalene triangle.

Solution:

```python
angle1 = int(input("Enter the first angle: "))
angle2 = int(input("Enter the second angle: "))
angle3 = int(input("Enter the third angle: "))

if angle1 == angle2 == angle3:
    print("Equilateral Triangle")
elif angle1 == angle2 or angle1 == angle3 or angle2 == angle3:
    print("Isosceles Triangle")
else:
    print("Scalene Triangle")
```

Exercise 7: Largest among Three Numbers

Description: Write a program that takes three numbers as input and prints the largest among them.

Solution:

```python
num1 = float(input("Enter the first number: "))
num2 = float(input("Enter the second number: "))
num3 = float(input("Enter the third number: "))

if num1 >= num2 and num1 >= num3:
    largest = num1
```

```
elif num2 >= num1 and num2 >= num3:

    largest = num2

else:

    largest = num3


print("The largest number is:", largest)
```

Exercise 8: Age Group

Description: Create a program that takes a person's age as input and prints their age group based on the following criteria:

0-12: Child
13-19: Teenager
20-59: Adult
60 and above: Senior

Solution:

```
age = int(input("Enter your age: "))
if age <= 12:
    age_group = "Child"
elif age <= 19:
    age_group = "Teenager"
elif age <= 59:
    age_group = "Adult"
else:
    age_group = "Senior"
print("You belong to the", age_group, "age group.")
```

Exercise 9: Calculator

Description: Write a program that takes two numbers and an operator (+, -, *, /) as input and performs the corresponding operation.

Solution:

```python
num1 = float(input("Enter the first number: "))
operator = input("Enter an operator (+, -, *, /): ")
num2 = float(input("Enter the second number: "))

if operator == "+":
    result = num1 + num2
elif operator == "-":
    result = num1 - num2
elif operator == "*":
    result = num1 * num2
elif operator == "/":
    result = num1 / num2
else:
    result = "Invalid operator"

print("Result:", result)
```

Exercise 10: Vowel or Consonant

Description: Create a program that takes a character (a letter) as input and prints whether it's a vowel or a consonant.

Solution:

```python
char = input("Enter a character: ").lower()
if char.isalpha() and len(char) == 1:
    if char in "aeiou":
        print("Vowel")
    else:
        print("Consonant")
else:
    print("Not a valid character.")
```

Lists and Tuples Exercises

These exercises cover basic operations with lists and tuples in Python, providing beginners with opportunities to practice working with these data structures.

Exercise 1: Create a List

Description: Write a Python program that creates a list of your favorite fruits and prints it.

Solution:
```
fruits = ["apple", "banana", "orange", "strawberry"]
print("My favorite fruits:", fruits)
```

Exercise 2: Access List Elements

Description: Create a program that accesses and prints the second element of a list.

Solution:

```
fruits = ["apple", "banana", "orange", "strawberry"]
print("Second fruit:", fruits[1])
```

Exercise 3: Append to List

Description: Write a program that appends a new fruit to the list of your favorite fruits and prints the updated list.

Solution:

```
fruits = ["apple", "banana", "orange", "strawberry"]
new_fruit = "grape"
fruits.append(new_fruit)
print("Updated list of favorite fruits:", fruits)
```

Exercise 4: List Slicing

Description: Create a program that slices and prints the first three elements of a list.

Solution:

```
fruits = ["apple", "banana", "orange", "strawberry"]
sliced_fruits = fruits[:3]
print("First three fruits:", sliced_fruits)
```

Exercise 5: Tuple Creation

Description: Write a Python program that creates a tuple containing the days of the week and prints it.

Solution:

```
days_of_week = ("Monday", "Tuesday", "Wednesday", "Thursday", "Friday",
"Saturday", "Sunday")
print("Days of the week:", days_of_week)
```

Exercise 6: Access Tuple Elements

Description: Create a program that accesses and prints the third day of the week from the tuple.

Solution:

```
days_of_week = ("Monday", "Tuesday", "Wednesday", "Thursday", "Friday",
"Saturday", "Sunday")
print("Third day of the week:", days_of_week[2])
```

Exercise 7: List Length

Description: Write a program that calculates and prints the number of elements in a list.

Solution:

```
fruits = ["apple", "banana", "orange", "strawberry"]
num_of_fruits = len(fruits)
print("Number of fruits:", num_of_fruits)
```

Exercise 8: Tuple Concatenation

Description: Create a program that concatenates two tuples containing days of the week and prints the resulting tuple.

Solution:

```
days1 = ("Monday", "Tuesday", "Wednesday")
days2 = ("Thursday", "Friday", "Saturday", "Sunday")
combined_days = days1 + days2

print("Combined days of the week:", combined_days)
```

Exercise 9: List Modification

Description: Write a program that modifies the second element of a list and prints the updated list.

Solution:

```
fruits = ["apple", "banana", "orange", "strawberry"]

fruits[1] = "kiwi"

print("Updated list of fruits:", fruits)
```

Exercise 10: Tuple Unpacking

Description: Create a program that unpacks a tuple containing a person's name and age and prints them separately.

Solution:

```
person_info = ("Alice", 30)

name, age = person_info

print("Name:", name)

print("Age:", age)
```

Loops Exercises.

These exercises provide practice in using for loops, while loops, and conditional statements in Python, making them suitable for beginners to build their programming skills.

Exercise 1: Print Numbers from 1 to 10

Description: Write a Python program that uses a for loop to print numbers from 1 to 10.

Solution:

```
for i in range(1, 11):

    print(i)
```

Exercise 2: Sum of Numbers

Description: Create a program that calculates and prints the sum of all numbers from 1 to 100.

Solution:

```
total = 0

for i in range(1, 101):

    total += i

print("Sum of numbers from 1 to 100:", total)
```

Exercise 3: Print Even Numbers

Description: Write a program that uses a for loop to print even numbers from 2 to 20.

Solution:

```
for i in range(2, 21, 2):

    print(i)
```

Exercise 4: Factorial Calculation

Description: Create a program that calculates and prints the factorial of a given number (e.g., 5! = 5 x 4 x 3 x 2 x 1).

Solution:

```python
num = int(input("Enter a number: "))

factorial = 1

for i in range(1, num + 1):

    factorial *= i

print(num, "! =", factorial)
```

Exercise 5: Multiplication Table

Description: Write a program that prints the multiplication table for a given number (e.g., 5 x 1 = 5, 5 x 2 = 10, ...).

Solution:

```python
num = int(input("Enter a number: "))

for i in range(1, 11):

    result = num * i

    print(num, "x", i, "=", result)
```

Exercise 6: Reverse a String

Description: Create a program that takes a string as input and prints it in reverse using a for loop.

Solution:

```python
text = input("Enter a string: ")

reversed_text = ""

for char in reversed(text):

    reversed_text += char

print("Reversed string:", reversed_text)
```

Exercise 7: Check Prime Number

Description: Write a program that checks if a given integer is a prime number.

Solution:

```python
num = int(input("Enter a number: "))
```

```python
    is_prime = True

    if num <= 1:

        is_prime = False

    else:

        for i in range(2, int(num**0.5) + 1):

            if num % i == 0:

                is_prime = False

                break

    if is_prime:

        print(num, "is a prime number.")

    else:

        print(num, "is not a prime number.")
```

Exercise 8: Print a Pattern

Description: Create a program that uses nested loops to print the following pattern:

```
*

**

***

****

*****
```

Solution:

```python
for i in range(1, 6):

    for j in range(i):

        print("*", end="")

    print()
```

Exercise 9: Fibonacci Series

Description: Write a program that prints the Fibonacci series up to a given number of terms.

Solution:

```python
num_terms = int(input("Enter the number of terms: "))

a, b = 0, 1

print("Fibonacci Series:")

for i in range(num_terms):

    print(a, end=" ")

    a, b = b, a + b
```

Exercise 10: Print Even Numbers using While Loop

Description: Create a program that uses a while loop to print even numbers from 2 to 20.

Solution:

```
num = 2

while num <= 20:

    print(num)

    num += 2
```

Dictionary Exercises.

These exercises introduce beginners to working with dictionaries in Python, allowing them to practice creating, accessing, and manipulating dictionary data.

Exercise 1: Create a Dictionary

Description: Write a Python program that creates a dictionary representing a person's information, including their name, age, and city.

Solution:

```
person = {
    "name": "Alice",
    "age": 30,
    "city": "New York"
}
print("Person's information:", person)
```

Exercise 2: Access Dictionary Values

Description: Create a program that accesses and prints the age of a person from the dictionary created in Exercise 1.

Solution:

```python
person = {
    "name": "Alice",
    "age": 30,
    "city": "New York"
}
print("Age:", person["age"])
```

Exercise 3: Add Key-Value Pair

Description: Write a program that adds a new key-value pair representing the person's email address to the dictionary.

Solution:

```python
person = {
    "name": "Alice",
    "age": 30,
    "city": "New York"
}
person["email"] = "alice@example.com"
print("Updated person's information:", person)
```

Exercise 4: Dictionary Length

Description: Create a program that calculates and prints the number of key-value pairs in the person's dictionary.

Solution:

```python
person = {
    "name": "Alice",
    "age": 30,
    "city": "New York"
}
num_items = len(person)
print("Number of key-value pairs:", num_items)
```

Exercise 5: Check for Key Existence

Description: Write a program that checks if a specific key (e.g., "email") exists in the person's dictionary and prints whether it exists or not.

Solution:

```python
person = {
    "name": "Alice",
    "age": 30,
    "city": "New York"
}
key_to_check = "email"
if key_to_check in person:
    print(key_to_check, "exists in the dictionary.")
else:
    print(key_to_check, "does not exist in the dictionary.")
```

Exercise 6: Iterate Through Keys

Description: Create a program that iterates through and prints all the keys in the person's dictionary.

Solution:

```python
person = {
    "name": "Alice",
    "age": 30,
    "city": "New York"
}
for key in person:
    print(key)
```

Exercise 7: Iterate Through Values

Description: Write a program that iterates through and prints all the values in the person's dictionary.

Solution:

```python
person = {
    "name": "Alice",
    "age": 30,
    "city": "New York"
}
for value in person.values():
    print(value)
```

Exercise 8: Iterate Through Key-Value Pairs

Description: Create a program that iterates through and prints all the key-value pairs in the person's dictionary.

Solution:

```python
person = {
    "name": "Alice",
    "age": 30,
    "city": "New York"
}
for key, value in person.items():
    print(key, ":", value)
```

Exercise 9: Remove Key-Value Pair

Description: Write a program that removes the "city" key-value pair from the person's dictionary and prints the updated dictionary.

Solution:

```python
person = {
    "name": "Alice",
    "age": 30,
    "city": "New York"
}
del person["city"]
print("Updated person's information:", person)
```

Exercise 10: Merge Dictionaries

Description: Create a program that merges two dictionaries, one representing personal information and another representing contact information, into a single dictionary.

Solution:

```python
personal_info = {
    "name": "Alice",
    "age": 30
}
contact_info = {
    "email": "alice@example.com",
    "phone": "123-456-7890"
}
merged_info = {**personal_info, **contact_info}
print("Merged information:", merged_info)
```

Functions Exercises.

These exercises provide beginners with opportunities to practice defining and using functions in Python to perform various tasks and calculations.

Exercise 1: Greet Function

Description: Write a Python function called greet that takes a name as an argument and prints a greeting message.

Solution:

```
def greet(name):
    print("Hello, " + name + "!")

# Calling the function
greet("Alice")
```

Exercise 2: Add Function

Description: Create a function called add that takes two numbers as arguments and returns their sum.

Solution:

```
def add(num1, num2):
```

```
        return num1 + num2

result = add(5, 3)
print("Sum:", result)
```

Exercise 3: Calculate Area of Circle

Description: Write a function called calculate_area that calculates and returns the area of a circle given its radius.

Solution:

```
import math

def calculate_area(radius):
    return math.pi * radius ** 2

area = calculate_area(3)
print("Area of the circle:", area)
```

Exercise 4: Check Even or Odd

Description: Create a function called is_even that takes an integer as an argument and returns True if it's even and False if it's odd.

Solution:

```
def is_even(number):
```

```
    return number % 2 == 0

result = is_even(4)
print("Is it even?", result)
```

Exercise 5: String Length Function

Description: Write a function called string_length that takes a string as an argument and returns its length.

Solution:

```
def string_length(text):
    return len(text)


length = string_length("Hello, World!")
print("Length of the string:", length)
```

Exercise 6: Check Leap Year Function

Description: Create a function called is_leap_year that checks if a year is a leap year and returns True or False.

Solution:

```
def is_leap_year(year):
    return (year % 4 == 0 and year % 100 != 0) or (year % 400 == 0)


result = is_leap_year(2024)
print("Is it a leap year?", result)
```

Exercise 7: Factorial Function

Description: Write a function called calculate_factorial that calculates and returns the factorial of a given number.

Solution:

```
def calculate_factorial(number):
    factorial = 1
    for i in range(1, number + 1):
        factorial *= i
    return factorial


result = calculate_factorial(5)
print("Factorial:", result)
```

Exercise 8: Reverse String Function

Description: Create a function called reverse_string that takes a string as an argument and returns the reverse of that string.

Solution:

```
def reverse_string(text):
    return text[::-1]


reversed_text = reverse_string("Python")
print("Reversed string:", reversed_text)
```

Exercise 9: Find Max Function

Description: Write a function called find_max that takes a list of numbers as an argument and returns the maximum number in the list.

Solution:

```
def find_max(numbers):
    return max(numbers)


numbers = [5, 8, 2, 10, 3]
max_number = find_max(numbers)
print("Maximum number:", max_number)
```

Exercise 10: Power Function

Description: Create a function called power that takes two numbers, base and exponent, as arguments and returns the result of raising the base to the exponent.

Solution:

```
def power(base, exponent):
    return base ** exponent


result = power(2, 3)
print("Result:", result)
```

Functional Programming Exercises.

These exercises introduce beginners to fundamental functional programming concepts in Python, such as map, filter, reduce, lambda functions, list comprehensions, and more.

Exercise 1: Map Function

Description: Write a Python program that uses the map function to square each element in a list of numbers and prints the squared values.

Solution:

```
numbers = [1, 2, 3, 4, 5]
squared_numbers = list(map(lambda x: x ** 2, numbers))
print("Squared numbers:", squared_numbers)
```

Exercise 2: Filter Function

Description: Create a program that uses the filter function to filter out even numbers from a list of integers and prints the filtered list.

Solution:

```python
numbers = [1, 2, 3, 4, 5, 6, 7, 8, 9, 10]
even_numbers = list(filter(lambda x: x % 2 == 0, numbers))
print("Even numbers:", even_numbers)
```

Exercise 3: Reduce Function

Description: Write a Python program that uses the reduce function to find the product of all elements in a list of numbers.

Solution:

```python
from functools import reduce

numbers = [1, 2, 3, 4, 5]
product = reduce(lambda x, y: x * y, numbers)
print("Product:", product)
```

Exercise 4: List Comprehension

Description: Create a program that uses list comprehension to generate a list of squared numbers from 1 to 10 and prints the list.

Solution:

```python
squared_numbers = [x ** 2 for x in range(1, 11)]
print("Squared numbers:", squared_numbers)
```

Exercise 5: Lambda Function

Description: Write a program that uses a lambda function to add 5 to a given number.

Solution:

```python
add_five = lambda x: x + 5
result = add_five(10)
print("Result:", result)
```

Exercise 6: Recursion - Factorial

Description: Create a program that calculates the factorial of a given number using a recursive function.

Solution:

```python
def factorial(n):
    if n == 0:
        return 1
    else:
```

```
        return n * factorial(n - 1)

result = factorial(5)
print("Factorial:", result)
```

Exercise 7: Higher-Order Function

Description: Write a program that defines a higher-order function called apply that takes a function and a list of numbers as arguments and applies the function to each element in the list, returning the results in a new list.

Solution:

```
def apply(func, numbers):
    return [func(x) for x in numbers]

numbers = [1, 2, 3, 4, 5]
squared_numbers = apply(lambda x: x ** 2, numbers)
print("Squared numbers:", squared_numbers)
```

Exercise 8: Currying

Description: Create a program that defines a curried function called add that takes two arguments and returns the sum. The curried function should be able to be called with one argument at a time.

Solution:

```python
def add(x):
    def add_x(y):
        return x + y
    return add_x


add_five = add(5)
result = add_five(10)
print("Result:", result)
```

Exercise 9: Partial Function

Description: Write a program that defines a function multiply that takes three arguments and returns the product. Then, use the functools.partial function to create a new function double that multiplies a number by 2.

Solution:

```python
from functools import partial

def multiply(x, y, z):
    return x * y * z

double = partial(multiply, 2)
result = double(5, 3)
print("Result:", result)
```

Exercise 10: Zip Function

Description: Create a program that uses the zip function to combine two lists, one containing names and another containing ages, into a list of tuples, and then prints the list of tuples.

Solution:

```
names = ["Alice", "Bob", "Charlie"]
ages = [25, 30, 35]
combined_data = list(zip(names, ages))
print("Combined data:", combined_data)
```

File and Directory Management Exercises.

These exercises cover basic file and directory management operations in Python and are suitable for beginners to practice working with files and directories.

Exercise 1: Create a Text File

Description: Write a Python program that creates a new text file named "my_file.txt" and writes "Hello, World!" into it.

Solution:

```python
# Open the file in write mode and write the text
with open("my_file.txt", "w") as file:
    file.write("Hello, World!")
```

Exercise 2: Read a Text File

Description: Create a program that reads and prints the contents of the "my_file.txt" created in Exercise 1.

Solution:

```python
# Open the file in read mode and read its contents
with open("my_file.txt", "r") as file:
    content = file.read()
```

```
    print(content)
```

Exercise 3: Append to a Text File

Description: Write a program that appends "This is a new line." to the end of the "my_file.txt" created in Exercise 1.

Solution:

```
# Open the file in append mode and write a new line
with open("my_file.txt", "a") as file:
    file.write("\nThis is a new line.")
```

Exercise 4: Create a Directory

Description: Create a Python program that creates a new directory named "my_directory."

Solution:

```
import os

# Create a directory
os.mkdir("my_directory")
```

Exercise 5: List Files in a Directory

Description: Write a program that lists all the files and directories in the current working directory.

Solution:

```python
import os

# List files and directories in the current working directory
contents = os.listdir(".")
print("Contents of the current directory:")
for item in contents:
    print(item)
```

Exercise 6: Copy a File

Description: Create a program that copies the "my_file.txt" created in Exercise 1 to a new file named "my_file_copy.txt."

Solution:

```python
import shutil

# Copy the file
shutil.copy("my_file.txt", "my_file_copy.txt")
```

Exercise 7: Rename a File

Description: Write a program that renames the "my_file.txt" to "renamed_file.txt."

Solution:

```
# Rename the file
os.rename("my_file.txt", "renamed_file.txt")
```

Exercise 8: Remove a File

Description: Create a program that deletes the "renamed_file.txt" created in Exercise 7.

Solution:

```
# Remove the file
os.remove("renamed_file.txt")
```

Exercise 9: Remove a Directory

Description: Write a program that removes the "my_directory" directory created in Exercise 4.

Solution:

```
# Remove the directory
os.rmdir("my_directory")
```

Exercise 10: Move a File

Description: Create a program that moves "my_file_copy.txt" to a new directory named "my_new_directory."

Solution:

```
# Create a new directory
os.mkdir("my_new_directory")
```

```
# Move the file to the new directory
shutil.move("my_file_copy.txt", "my_new_directory/my_file_copy.txt")
```

Debugging Exercises.

These exercises cover common debugging scenarios and help beginners practice identifying and fixing errors in Python code.

Exercise 1: Syntax Error

Description: The following code has a syntax error. Find and fix it.

```python
print("Hello, World!")
```

Solution:

```python
print("Hello, World!")
```

Exercise 2: Indentation Error

Description: The code below contains an indentation error. Correct the indentation.

```python
def greet():
print("Hello!")

greet()
```

Solution:

```python
def greet():
    print("Hello!")

greet()
```

Exercise 3: Undefined Variable

Description: Identify and fix the error in the code below. The variable name is not defined.

```
print("Hello, " + name)
```

```
Solution:
name = "Alice"
print("Hello, " + name)
```

Exercise 4: Division by Zero

Description: Find and handle the division by zero error in the code below.

```
numerator = 10
denominator = 0
result = numerator / denominator
print("Result:", result)
```

Solution:

```
numerator = 10
denominator = 0

if denominator != 0:
    result = numerator / denominator
    print("Result:", result)
else:
    print("Cannot divide by zero.")
```

Exercise 5: Type Error

Description: The code below has a type error. Fix it so that it adds two numbers correctly.

```
num1 = "5"
num2 = 3
result = num1 + num2
print("Result:", result)
```

Solution:

```
num1 = "5"
num2 = 3
result = int(num1) + num2
print("Result:", result)
```

Exercise 6: Index Error

Description: Correct the index error in the code below. The list has only one element.

```
fruits = ["apple"]
print(fruits[1])
```

```
Solution:
fruits = ["apple"]
print(fruits[0])
```

Exercise 7: Name Error

Description: The variable age is referenced before it's defined. Fix this issue.

```
print("You are " + age + " years old.")
age = 25
```

Solution:

```
age = 25
print("You are " + str(age) + " years old.")
```

Exercise 8: Debugging with Print

Description: Use print statements to debug the following code and find the issue.

```
for i in range(5):
    print(i)
    print(10 / i)
```

Solution:

```
for i in range(1, 5):
    print(i)
    print(10 / i)
```

Exercise 9: Infinite Loop

Description: Identify and fix the issue causing an infinite loop in the code below.

```
num = 5
while num > 0:
    print(num)
```

Solution:

```
num = 5
while num > 0:
    print(num)
    num -= 1
```

Exercise 10: ValueError Handling

Description: Add exception handling to handle a ValueError when converting user input to an integer.

```
user_input = input("Enter a number: ")
num = int(user_input)
print("You entered:", num)
```

Solution:

```python
user_input = input("Enter a number: ")

try:
    num = int(user_input)
    print("You entered:", num)
except ValueError:
    print("Invalid input. Please enter a valid number.")
```

Pandas Libraries Exercises.

These exercises provide beginners with a hands-on introduction to basic operations and concepts in Pandas, making it easier to work with data in Python.

Exercise 1: Import Pandas

Description: Write a Python program that imports the Pandas library and prints "Pandas is imported successfully" if it's imported correctly.

Solution:

```
import pandas as pd

print("Pandas is imported successfully")
```

Exercise 2: Creating a DataFrame

Description: Create a simple Pandas DataFrame with two columns: "Name" and "Age," and populate it with data for three people.

Solution:

```
import pandas as pd

data = {"Name": ["Alice", "Bob", "Charlie"], "Age": [25, 30, 35]}
df = pd.DataFrame(data)
print(df)
```

Exercise 3: Loading CSV Data

Description: Load a CSV file named "data.csv" into a Pandas DataFrame and print the first five rows.

Solution:

```
import pandas as pd

df = pd.read_csv("data.csv")
print(df.head())
```

Exercise 4: Basic DataFrame Operations

Description: Perform basic DataFrame operations: select the "Name" column, calculate the mean age, and count the number of rows.

Solution:

```
import pandas as pd

data = {"Name": ["Alice", "Bob", "Charlie"], "Age": [25, 30, 35]}
df = pd.DataFrame(data)

name_column = df["Name"]
mean_age = df["Age"].mean()
num_rows = len(df)
```

```
print("Name Column:")
print(name_column)
print("Mean Age:", mean_age)
print("Number of Rows:", num_rows)
```

Exercise 5: Filtering Data

Description: Filter the rows in a DataFrame where the age is greater than 30.

Solution:

```
import pandas as pd

data = {"Name": ["Alice", "Bob", "Charlie"], "Age": [25, 30, 35]}
df = pd.DataFrame(data)

filtered_df = df[df["Age"] > 30]
print(filtered_df)
```

Exercise 6: Sorting Data

Description: Sort a DataFrame by the "Age" column in ascending order.

Solution:

```
import pandas as pd

data = {"Name": ["Alice", "Bob", "Charlie"], "Age": [25, 30, 35]}
df = pd.DataFrame(data)

sorted_df = df.sort_values(by="Age")
```

```
print(sorted_df)
```

Exercise 7: Grouping Data

Description: Group a DataFrame by the "Age" column and calculate the mean age for each group.

Solution:

```
import pandas as pd

data = {"Name": ["Alice", "Bob", "Charlie"], "Age": [25, 30, 35]}
df = pd.DataFrame(data)

grouped = df.groupby("Age")["Age"].mean()
print(grouped)
```

Exercise 8: Adding a New Column

Description: Add a new column "Gender" to a DataFrame and populate it with gender values for the three people.

Solution:

```
import pandas as pd

data = {"Name": ["Alice", "Bob", "Charlie"], "Age": [25, 30, 35]}
df = pd.DataFrame(data)

df["Gender"] = ["Female", "Male", "Male"]
print(df)
```

Exercise 9: Saving Data to CSV

Description: Save a DataFrame to a CSV file named "output.csv."

Solution:

```
import pandas as pd

data = {"Name": ["Alice", "Bob", "Charlie"], "Age": [25, 30, 35]}
df = pd.DataFrame(data)

df.to_csv("output.csv", index=False)
```

Exercise 10: Basic DataFrame Information

Description: Load a CSV file named "data.csv" into a DataFrame and print basic information about the DataFrame, including column names, data types, and summary statistics.

Solution:

```
import pandas as pd

df = pd.read_csv("data.csv")

print("Column Names:")
print(df.columns)

print("\nData Types:")
print(df.dtypes)

print("\nSummary Statistics:")
print(df.describe())
```

Matplotlib Library Exercises.

These exercises provide beginners with hands-on practice in creating various types of plots using the Matplotlib library and customizing their appearance.

Exercise 1: Importing Matplotlib

Description: Write a Python program that imports the Matplotlib library and prints "Matplotlib is imported successfully" if it's imported correctly.

Solution:

import matplotlib.pyplot as plt

print("Matplotlib is imported successfully")

Exercise 2: Creating a Basic Plot

Description: Create a basic line plot using Matplotlib to display the following data points: (1, 2), (2, 4), (3, 1), (4, 5).

Solution:

```
import matplotlib.pyplot as plt

x = [1, 2, 3, 4]
y = [2, 4, 1, 5]

plt.plot(x, y)
```

```
plt.xlabel("X-axis")
plt.ylabel("Y-axis")
plt.title("Basic Line Plot")
plt.show()
```

Exercise 3: Scatter Plot

Description: Create a scatter plot using Matplotlib to visualize the following data points: (1, 2), (2, 4), (3, 1), (4, 5).

Solution:

```
import matplotlib.pyplot as plt

x = [1, 2, 3, 4]
y = [2, 4, 1, 5]

plt.scatter(x, y)
plt.xlabel("X-axis")
plt.ylabel("Y-axis")
plt.title("Scatter Plot")
plt.show()
```

Exercise 4: Bar Chart

Description: Create a bar chart using Matplotlib to represent the following data: Categories - ["A", "B", "C", "D"], Values - [10, 15, 7, 12].

```
Solution:
import matplotlib.pyplot as plt

categories = ["A", "B", "C", "D"]
values = [10, 15, 7, 12]
```

```
plt.bar(categories, values)
plt.xlabel("Categories")
plt.ylabel("Values")
plt.title("Bar Chart")
plt.show()
```

Exercise 5: Histogram

Description: Generate a histogram using Matplotlib for a list of exam scores: [85, 92, 88, 78, 95, 89, 76, 94, 90, 82].

Solution:

```
import matplotlib.pyplot as plt

scores = [85, 92, 88, 78, 95, 89, 76, 94, 90, 82]

plt.hist(scores, bins=5, edgecolor='black')
plt.xlabel("Score Range")
plt.ylabel("Frequency")
plt.title("Histogram of Exam Scores")
plt.show()
```

Exercise 6: Pie Chart

Description: Create a pie chart using Matplotlib to represent the distribution of fruit types: ["Apples", "Bananas", "Cherries", "Dates"] with corresponding quantities: [30, 45, 15, 20].

Solution:

```python
import matplotlib.pyplot as plt

fruits = ["Apples", "Bananas", "Cherries", "Dates"]
quantities = [30, 45, 15, 20]

plt.pie(quantities, labels=fruits, autopct='%1.1f%%', startangle=140)
plt.axis('equal')
plt.title("Pie Chart of Fruit Distribution")
plt.show()
```

Exercise 7: Multiple Plots

Description: Create a figure with two subplots. In one subplot, plot a line graph of (1, 2, 3, 4) against (2, 4, 1, 5). In the other subplot, plot a bar chart of ["A", "B", "C", "D"] against [10, 15, 7, 12].

Solution:

```python
import matplotlib.pyplot as plt

# Data for the first subplot
x1 = [1, 2, 3, 4]
y1 = [2, 4, 1, 5]

# Data for the second subplot
categories = ["A", "B", "C", "D"]
values = [10, 15, 7, 12]

# Create a figure with two subplots
plt.figure(figsize=(10, 4))
```

```
plt.subplot(1, 2, 1)
plt.plot(x1, y1)
plt.xlabel("X-axis")
plt.ylabel("Y-axis")
plt.title("Line Plot")


plt.subplot(1, 2, 2)
plt.bar(categories, values)
plt.xlabel("Categories")
plt.ylabel("Values")
plt.title("Bar Chart")


plt.tight_layout()
plt.show()
```

Exercise 8: Customizing Plot Appearance

Description: Create a line plot of (1, 2, 3, 4) against (2, 4, 1, 5) with a red dashed line, green triangles as markers, and a legend.

Solution:

```
import matplotlib.pyplot as plt

x = [1, 2, 3, 4]
y = [2, 4, 1, 5]

plt.plot(x, y, 'r--', marker='^', label='Data')
plt.xlabel("X-axis")
plt.ylabel("Y-axis")
plt.title("Customized Line Plot")
plt.legend()
plt.show()
```

Exercise 9: Saving a Plot

Description: Generate a line plot of (1, 2, 3, 4) against (2, 4, 1, 5) and save it as a PNG image named "line_plot.png."

Solution:

```
import matplotlib.pyplot as plt

x = [1, 2, 3, 4]
y = [2, 4, 1, 5]

plt.plot(x, y)
plt.xlabel("X-axis")
plt.ylabel("Y-axis")
plt.title("Line Plot")
plt.savefig("line_plot.png")
```

Exercise 10: Subplots Grid

Description: Create a 2x2 grid of subplots, each containing a bar chart of ["A", "B", "C", "D"] against [10, 15, 7, 12]. Customize each subplot with different colors.

Solution:

```python
import matplotlib.pyplot as plt

categories = ["A", "B", "C", "D"]
values = [10, 15, 7, 12]

fig, axes = plt.subplots(2, 2, figsize=(10, 6))

colors = ['r', 'g', 'b', 'y']

for i, ax in enumerate(axes.flat):
    ax.bar(categories, values, color=colors[i])
    ax.set_xlabel("Categories")
    ax.set_ylabel("Values")
    ax.set_title(f"Subplot {i+1}")

plt.tight_layout()
plt.show()
```